BIBLE ANIMALS

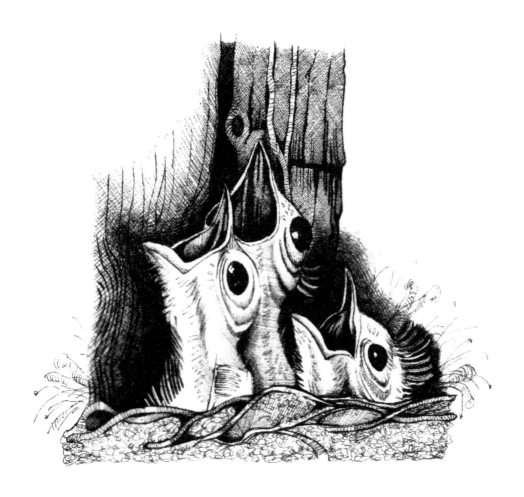

Lessons on living for God,
based on some Bible birds and animals.

THE BANNER OF TRUTH TRUST

THE BANNER OF TRUTH TRUST

3 Murrayfield Road, Edinburgh EH12 6EL, UK
P.O. Box 621, Carlisle, PA 17013, USA

*

© Alison Brown 2012

ISBN: 978 1 84871 179 2

*

Typeset in Myriad Pro 22/26.4 pt at
The Banner of Truth Trust,
Edinburgh

Printed in the USA by
Versa Press Inc.,
East Peoria, IL

*

Inspired by
a little girl's life-long
love affair with animals . . .
my daughter Hannah.

Birds and animals are often mentioned in Scripture. As we think about them we can learn many lessons about being a child of God, and living for him. Let's start at the beginning of the Bible . . .

A Sly Serpent

One very well known animal we read about in the Bible appeared in the Garden of Eden. When Satan came to tempt Eve, he disguised himself by appearing as a serpent.

God punishes Sin

Sadly, Eve listened to the lies of the serpent and sinned against God (Genesis 3).

God always judges sin. He cannot ignore it because he is holy. He punished Eve and he cursed the serpent. God said that from then on it would have to slither over the ground on its belly and eat dust!

A Careful Dove

When the raging flood waters were going down Noah wondered just when he should leave the ark. First he sent out a raven, and later . . . a dove (Genesis 8).

During the flood there may have been animal bodies floating in the water, and ravens are happy to feed on rotting meat.

But the gentle dove came back to the safety of the ark to find a clean place to rest.

What is Sin?

We too need to be able to tell the difference between things which are clean, and things which are unclean.

Sinful things are those which make little of God or his commandments, or turn our thoughts against him.

A Perfect Ram

God tested Abraham by asking him to offer up his son Isaac on an altar, as a love gift to God (Genesis 22). But just as obedient Abraham was about to do it God stopped him. Abraham had shown that he loved God above everything else. He was very thankful to find a ram (caught by its horns in a nearby bush), which was unhurt and perfect. God had provided the ram for him to use as a sacrifice instead.

A Sacrifice for Sin

God later sent *his own* Son Jesus, not just as a love gift to the world, but to give his life as the only sacrifice for sin!

Jesus was the only one who could do this because he was not the son of Joseph, but of God — so he had no sins of his own to pay for. When we repent of our sin and believe in Jesus, who was punished in our place, God will give us everlasting life, just as he promised (John 3:16).

Thirsty Camels

Rebekah was a kind and thoughtful girl. She met a stranger at the well who had ten thirsty camels. They had all travelled many, many miles. So Rebekah drew enough water from the well to give the tired man and all his camels a drink. She knew that after walking through a dusty desert nothing else would satisfy their thirst (Genesis 24).

The Water Of Life

We are just like those thirsty camels. We long to feel satisfied. We sometimes think that buying more things will make us happy, but true joy comes through trusting in Jesus. Jesus said, 'Whoever drinks of the water that I shall give him shall never thirst' (John 4:14).

Spotted Goats

For many years Jacob had worked, as a shepherd, for Laban, his father-in-law (Genesis 31). Now it was time to go home. To thank him for all his work, Laban said he could have all the spotted goats and brown lambs. God had promised to bless Jacob so he caused many of the new kids and lambs to be born spotted, speckled and brown!

God will Provide

Soon Jacob had a large flock. The animals were not white but there were hundreds of them!

God has promised to take care of those who take Jesus as their Saviour and become children of God. He may not always give them what they want or wish for, but he will always supply their needs.

Hopping Frogs

In Exodus 8:1-15 we read about frogs leaping through the homes of the Egyptians! Thousands of frogs came up from the River Nile and hopped through the bedrooms and kitchens! God caused it to happen.

He was
showing the
people of Egypt that
he was much more
powerful than all their false gods.
God alone has power over all that he has created.

God is in Control

In the beginning God created a perfect world.
There were no famines, earthquakes, or diseases then.
But after Adam
and Eve sinned
against God
everything
changed.

The curse
of sin was
sorrow,
pain,
decay,
and death.

Accidents, illness,
and disasters happen
naturally in our sin-spoiled world today. Sometimes God
prevents them when his children obey him and pray to
him for help. God can protect us, just as he protected
the Israelites, when he brought terrible plagues upon the
Egyptians. God can cause nature, and animals, and the
weather to do just as he pleases!

A Snarling Bear

When David was just a shepherd boy he came face to face with a thieving bear!

The bear had come to snatch a lamb from among his flock of sheep.

God helped David to overcome the bear, and rescue the lamb! God used the wild animals David fought with to teach him to trust God in times of great danger. David would need to learn that very important lesson before he met the giant Goliath (1 Samuel 17:34-37)!

Trust in God

We may never meet a snarling bear but sometimes we can face frightening things, or people, or situations. God wants us to look up to him and trust him completely when we feel afraid.

Busy Birds

God's prophet Elijah had been a faithful messenger for God. But wicked Queen Jezebel did not like him. She wanted to have him killed, and Elijah didn't know where to go, or how to escape.

God told
him just
what to do.

God sent him to hide
in a ravine, beside a little brook called Cherith, and promised to send ravens to feed him! Elijah must have wondered how God would do this. Nevertheless, he listened to God's words and did just as he was told.

Listen to God

It would have been easy for Elijah to have doubted the wisdom of God, and his unusual instructions, but he didn't. God kept him perfectly safe (1 Kings 17:1-6).

As we read the Bible
we need to learn to listen to God's voice.
We may not always understand why God wants us to do as he says, but if we listen to his wise words, rather than our own ideas, he will bless us.

Hungry Lions

The lions must have roared with delight just before Daniel was thrown into their den. But then God sent an angel to close their mouths. God protected Daniel because Daniel had faithfully continued to pray to him, even though he knew he could lose his life (Daniel 6).

Talk to God

God loves to hear his children pray. We cannot get to know God better unless we talk with him. God wants us to express our thankfulness and explain our fears, just as Daniel did. God has promised to answer the prayers of those who obey him.

A Monstrous Whale

Jonah was not an obedient prophet. God told him to go to the city of Nineveh to warn the people there about God's coming judgement on them, but he refused.

Instead he ran away and tried to hide from God by taking a ship in another direction! But God knew exactly where he was and sent a raging storm. Jonah knew he had done wrong when he was thrown overboard!

Obey God

Jonah learned his lesson in a painful way (Jonah 2:5). He almost drowned before being swallowed by a huge fish, or whale, which God mercifully sent to rescue him. If he had obeyed at the beginning he would never have been down at the bottom of the sea with the weeds wrapped around his head! We can learn an important lesson from this story. God only blesses obedience.

Grubby Pigs

The prodigal son came from a wealthy home. He turned his back on it all and left home because he thought the world looked much more exciting. He wanted to please himself and live by his own rules (Luke 15).

He wasted all of his inheritance and grieved his father. He ended up with no possessions and no friends. He had to feed pigs . . . and eat pig-food to stay alive!

Confess our Sin

But the prodigal son didn't stay there. He realized that he had sinned. He went back to his father and humbly said sorry. His father, who loved him dearly, forgave him.

If we sin we need to go back to God and do the same. If we mean what we say God will forgive us.

Grazing Sheep

In John 10:1-5 Jesus described how sheep followed their shepherd to new pastures.

In Israel a shepherd did not drive his sheep from behind. Instead, he walked in front, calling his own sheep by name. The sheep would only follow a voice they knew. If a strange voice called them, they refused to go.

Follow Jesus

There are many strange voices in the world today, which call us to trust the ideas of men, instead of God's Word.

A believer will be led by Jesus, the Good Shepherd (John 10:14). As we obey him, he will guide us to the places he has chosen. We will never be alone because Jesus always walks in front . . . and he knows the best path!

An Untrained Colt

When Jesus rode into Jerusalem, to celebrate the Feast of the Passover, he didn't ride on a white horse, like a king going into battle. Instead he used a young donkey (Mark 11:1-11).

That donkey had never been ridden before. It was not used to having a load on its back. It had never carried a person anywhere! But Jesus had a reason for using it, and by his power, it became a very useful animal.

Serve the King

Hundreds of years before this, the prophets had written that the King who would bring salvation would come to Jerusalem on the foal of a donkey (Zechariah 9:9). The time had now come for Jesus to use this young colt.

God may ask you to do something which no-one else can do. God can do big and wonderful things through people who know they are little, and need God's help!

A Crowing Rooster

The day before Jesus, the Son of God, was crucified, he spoke with his disciple Peter (Luke 22:33-72).

He told Peter that before the cock would crow in the morning, he would say that he was not a friend of Jesus.

And that is just what happened. Peter said that he knew nothing at all about the prisoner who had been arrested in Gethsemane.

He did not want anyone to know that he was a friend of Jesus in case he would be put in chains too!

Be Loyal to Jesus

Later, after Jesus had risen from the dead to life again, he forgave Peter (John 21:15-19).

Peter went on to show true love for Jesus by spending the rest of his life telling others about him.

He was no longer ashamed to know Jesus!

We too must not be afraid to tell our friends the very wonderful news, that the Son of God came down to earth to make a way for sinful people to go to heaven!

Talking Time

Being a Christian will affect every part of your life . . . but Jesus gave *all* of his life for you. What truths can you remember now, as you look at each creature below?